'It is a most wonderful comfort to sit alone beneath a lamp, book spread before you, and commune with someone from the past whom you never met.'

YOSHIDA KENKŌ
Born *c*. 1283, Japan
Died *c*. 1352, Japan

Selection taken from *Essays in Idleness* (*Tsurezuregusa*), which
was probably written around 1329–31.

KENKŌ IN PENGUIN CLASSICS
Essays in Idleness and *Hōjōki*

YOSHIDA KENKŌ

A Cup of Sake Beneath the Cherry Trees

Translated by
Meredith McKinney

PENGUIN BOOKS

PENGUIN CLASSICS

Published by the Penguin Group
Penguin Books Ltd, 80 Strand, London wc2r orl, England
Penguin Group (USA) Inc., 375 Hudson Street, New York, New York 10014, USA
Penguin Group (Canada), 90 Eglinton Avenue East, Suite 700, Toronto, Ontario,
Canada m4p 2y3 (a division of Pearson Penguin Canada Inc.)
Penguin Ireland, 25 St Stephen's Green, Dublin 2, Ireland
(a division of Penguin Books Ltd)
Penguin Group (Australia), 707 Collins Street, Melbourne, Victoria 3008, Australia
(a division of Pearson Australia Group Pty Ltd)
Penguin Books India Pvt Ltd, 11 Community Centre, Panchsheel Park,
New Delhi – 110 017, India
Penguin Group (NZ), 67 Apollo Drive, Rosedale, Auckland 0632, New Zealand
(a division of Pearson New Zealand Ltd)
Penguin Books (South Africa) (Pty) Ltd, Block D, Rosebank Office Park,
181 Jan Smuts Avenue, Parktown North, Gauteng 2193, South Africa

Penguin Books Ltd, Registered Offices: 80 Strand, London wc2r orl, England

www.penguin.com

This selection published in Penguin Classics 2015
002

Translation copyright © Meredith McKinney, 2013
The moral right of the translator has been asserted

Set in 9.5/13 pt Baskerville 10 Pro
Typeset by Jouve (UK), Milton Keynes
Printed in Great Britain by Clays Ltd, St Ives plc

A CIP catalogue record for this book is available from the British Library

isbn: 978–0–141–39825–9

www.greenpenguin.co.uk

MIX
Paper from
responsible sources
FSC® C018179
www.fsc.org

Penguin Books is committed to a sustainable
future for our business, our readers and our planet.
This book is made from Forest Stewardship
Council™ certified paper.

Preface

What strange folly, to beguile the tedious hours like this all day before my ink stone, jotting down at random the idle thoughts that cross my mind . . .

*

To be born into this world of ours, it seems, brings with it so much to long for.

The rank of emperor is, of course, unspeakably exalted; even his remotest descendants fill one with awe, having sprung from no mere human seed.

Needless to say, the great ruler, and even the lesser nobles who are granted attendant guards to serve them, are also thoroughly magnificent. Their children and grandchildren too are still impressive, even if they have come down in the world. As for those of lesser degree, although they may make good according to their rank, and put on airs and consider themselves special, they are really quite pathetic.

No one could be less enviable than a monk. Sei

Shōnagon wrote that people treat them like unfeeling lumps of wood, and this is perfectly true. And there is nothing impressive about the way those with power will throw their weight around. As the holy man Sōga, I think, remarked, fame and fortune are an affliction for a monk, and violate the Buddha's teachings.

There is much to admire, though, in a dedicated recluse.

It is most important to present well, in both appearance and bearing. One never tires of spending time with someone whose speech is attractive and pleasing to the ear, and who does not talk overmuch. There is nothing worse than when someone you thought impressive reveals himself as lacking in sensibility. Status and personal appearance are things one is born with, after all, but surely the inner man can always be improved with effort. It is a great shame to see a fine upstanding fellow fall in with low and ugly types who easily run rings round him, and all for want of cultivation and learning.

A man should learn the orthodox literature, write poetry in Chinese as well as Japanese, and study music, and should ideally also be a model to others in his familiarity with ceremonial court customs and precedents. He should write a smooth, fair hand, carry the rhythm well when songs are sung at banquets, and when offered sake, make a show of declining it but nevertheless be able to drink.

*

No matter how splendid in every way, there is something dreadfully lacking in a man who does not pursue the art of love. He is, to coin the old phrase, like a beautiful wine cup that lacks a base.

The elegant thing is for a lover to wander aimlessly hither and yon, drenched with the frosts or dews of night, tormented by fears of his parents' reproaches and the censure of the world, the heart beset with uncertainties, yet for all that sleeping often alone, though always fitfully.

On the other hand, he shouldn't lose himself to love too thoroughly, or gain the reputation of being putty in women's hands.

*

If our life did not fade and vanish like the dews of Adashino's graves or the drifting smoke from Toribe's burning grounds, but lingered on for ever, how little the world would move us. It is the ephemeral nature of things that makes them wonderful.

Among all living creatures, it is man that lives longest. The brief dayfly dies before evening; summer's cicada knows neither spring nor autumn. What a glorious luxury it is to taste life to the full for even a single year. If you constantly regret life's passing, even a thousand long years will seem but the dream of a night.

Why cling to a life which cannot last for ever, only

to arrive at ugly old age? The longer you live, the greater your share of shame. It is most seemly to die before forty at the latest. Once past this age, people develop an urge to mix with others without the least shame at their own unsightliness; they spend their dwindling years fussing adoringly over their children and grand-children, hoping to live long enough to see them make good in the world. Their greed for the things of this world grows ever deeper, till they lose all ability to be moved by life's pathos, and become really quite disgraceful.

*

Nothing so distracts the human heart as sexual desire. How foolish men's hearts are!

Aroma, for instance, is a mere transient thing, yet a whiff of delightful incense from a woman's robes will always excite a man, though he knows perfectly well that it is just a passing effect of robe-smoking.

The wizard priest of Kume is said to have lost his supernatural powers when he spied the white legs of a woman as she squatted washing clothes. I can quite believe it – after all, the beautiful, plump, glowing flesh of a woman's arm or leg is quite a different matter from some artificial allurement.

*

Beautiful hair on a woman will draw a man's gaze – but we can judge what manner of person she is and the nature of her sensibility even by simply hearing her speak from behind a screen. A mere unintended glimpse of a woman can distract a man's heart; and if a woman sleeps fitfully, and is prepared to endure impossible difficulties heedless of her own well-being, it is all because her mind is on love.

Yes indeed, the ways of love lie deep in us. Many are the allurements of our senses, yet we can distance ourselves from them all. But among them this one alone seems without exception to plague us all, young and old, wise and foolish.

So it is that we have those tales of how a woman's hair can snare and hold even an elephant, or how the rutting stag of autumn will always be drawn by the sound of a flute made from the wood of a woman's shoe.

We must discipline ourselves to be constantly prudent and vigilant lest we fall into this trap.

*

Though a home is of course merely a transient habitation, a place that is set up in beautiful taste to suit its owner is a delightful thing.

Even the moonlight is so much the more moving when it shines into a house where a refined person dwells in tranquil elegance. There is nothing fashionable or showy about the place, it is true, yet the grove of trees is redolent

5

of age, the plants in the carefully untended garden carry a hint of delicate feelings, while the veranda and open-weave fence are tastefully done, and inside the house the casually disposed things have a tranquil, old-fashioned air. It is all most refined.

How ugly and depressing to see a house that has employed a bevy of craftsmen to work everything up to a fine finish, where all the household items set out for proud display are rare and precious foreign or Japanese objects, and where even the plants in the garden are clipped and contorted rather than left to grow as they will. How could anyone live for long in such a place? The merest glimpse will provoke the thought that all this could go up in smoke in an instant.

Yes, on the whole you can tell a great deal about the owner from his home.

The Later Tokudaiji Minister once had rope strung over the roof of the main house to stop the kites from roosting on it. 'What could be wrong with having kites on your roof? This shows what manner of man he is!' exclaimed the poet-monk Saigyō, and it is said he never called there again. I was reminded of this story when I noticed once that Prince Ayanokōji had laid rope over his Kosaka residence. Someone told me, however, that it was because he pitied the frogs in his pond when he observed how crows gathered on the roof to catch them. I was most impressed. Perhaps the Tokudaiji Minister too might have had some such reason for acting as he did?

*

One day in the tenth month, I went to call on someone in a remote mountain village beyond Kurusuno.

Making my way along the mossy path, I came at length to the lonely hut where he lived. There was not a sound except for the soft drip of water from a bamboo pipe buried deep in fallen leaves. The vase on the altar shelf with its haphazard assortment of chrysanthemums and sprigs of autumn leaves bespoke someone's presence.

Moved, I said to myself, 'One could live like this' – but my mood was then somewhat spoiled by noticing at the far end of the garden a large mandarin tree, branches bowed with fruit, that was firmly protected by a stout fence. If only that tree weren't there! I thought.

*

What happiness to sit in intimate conversation with someone of like mind, warmed by candid discussion of the amusing and fleeting ways of this world . . . but such a friend is hard to find, and instead you sit there doing your best to fit in with whatever the other is saying, feeling deeply alone.

There is some pleasure to be had from agreeing with the other in general talk that interests you both, but it's better if he takes a slightly different position from yours. 'No, I can't agree with that,' you'll say to each other

7

combatively, and you'll fall into arguing the matter out. This sort of lively discussion is a pleasant way to pass the idle hours, but in fact most people tend to grumble about things different from oneself, and though you can put up with the usual boring platitudes, such men are far indeed from the true friend after your own heart, and leave you feeling quite forlorn.

*

It is a most wonderful comfort to sit alone beneath a lamp, book spread before you, and commune with someone from the past whom you have never met.

As to books – those moving volumes of *Wenxuan*, the *Wenji* of Bai Juyi, the words of Laozi and *Zhuangzi*. There are many moving works from our own land, too, by scholars of former times.

*

It is an excellent thing to live modestly, shun luxury and wealth and not lust after fame and fortune. Rare has been the wise man who was rich.

In China once there was a man by the name of Xu You, who owned nothing and even drank directly from his cupped hands. Seeing this, someone gave him a 'singing gourd' to use as a cup; he hung it in a tree, but when he heard it singing in the wind one day he threw it away, annoyed by the noise it made, and went back to drinking his water from his hands. What a free, pure spirit!

Sun Chen had no bedclothes to sleep under in the winter months, only a bundle of straw which he slept in at night and put away again each morning.

The Chinese wrote these stories to hand down to later times because they found them so impressive. No one bothers to tell such tales in our country.

*

The changing seasons are moving in every way.

Everyone seems to feel that 'it is above all autumn that moves the heart to tears', and there is some truth in this, yet surely it is spring that stirs the heart more profoundly. Then, birdsong is full of the feel of spring, the plants beneath the hedges bud into leaf in the warm sunlight, the slowly deepening season brings soft mists, while the blossoms at last begin to open, only to meet with ceaseless winds and rain that send them flurrying restlessly to earth. Until the leaves appear on the boughs, the heart is endlessly perturbed.

The scented flowering orange is famously evocative, but it is above all plum blossom that has the power to carry you back to moments of cherished memory. The exquisite kerria, the hazy clusters of wisteria blossom – all these things linger in the heart.

Someone has said that at the time of the Buddha's birthday and the Kamo festival in the fourth month, when

9

the trees are cool with luxuriant new leaf, one is particularly moved by the pathos of things and by a longing for others, and indeed it is true. And who could not be touched to melancholy in the fifth month, when the sweet flag iris leaves are laid on roofs, and the rice seedlings are planted out, and the water rail's knocking call is heard? The sixth month is also moving, with white evening-glory blooming over the walls of poor dwellings, and the smoke from smouldering smudge fires. The purifications of the sixth month are also delightful.

The festival of Tanabata is wonderfully elegant. Indeed so many things happen together in autumn – the nights grow slowly more chill, wild geese come crying over, and when the bush clover begins to yellow the early rice is harvested and hung to dry. The morning after a typhoon has blown through is also delightful.

Writing this, I realize that all this has already been spoken of long ago in *The Tale of Genji* and *The Pillow Book* – but that is no reason not to say it again. After all, things thought but left unsaid only fester inside you. So I let my brush run on like this for my own foolish solace; these pages deserve to be torn up and discarded, after all, and are not something others will ever see.

To continue – the sight of a bare wintry landscape is almost as lovely as autumn. It is delightful to see fallen autumn leaves scattered among the plants by the water's edge, or vapour rising from the garden stream on a morning white with frost. It is also especially moving to observe everyone bustling about at year's end, preparing for the new year. And then there is the forlornly touching sight of the waning moon around the twentieth day, hung in a clear, cold sky, although people consider it too dreary to look at. The Litany of Buddha Names and the Presentation of Tributes are thoroughly moving and magnificent, and in fact all the numerous court ceremonies and events at around this time, taking place as they do amidst the general end-of-year bustle, present an impressive sight. The way the Worship of the Four Directions follows so quickly upon the Great Demon Expulsion is wonderful too.

In the thick darkness of New Year's Eve, people light pine torches and rush about, so fast that their feet virtually skim the ground, making an extraordinary racket for some reason, and knocking on everyone's doors until late at night – but then at last around dawn all grows quiet, and you savour the touching moment of saying farewell to the old year. I was moved to find that in the East they still perform the ritual for dead souls on the night when the dead are said to return, although these days this has ceased to be done in the capital.

And so, watching the new year dawn in the sky, you are stirred by a sense of utter newness, although the sky looks no different from yesterday's. It is also touching to see the happy sight of new year pines gaily decorating the houses all along the main streets.

*

A certain recluse monk once remarked, 'I have relinquished all that ties me to the world, but the one thing that still haunts me is the beauty of the sky.' I can quite see why he would feel this.

*

How mutable the flower of the human heart, a fluttering blossom gone before the breeze's touch – so we recall the bygone years when the heart of another was our close companion, each dear word that stirred us then still unforgotten; and yet, it is the way of things that the beloved should move into worlds beyond our own, a parting far sadder than from the dead. Thus did Mozi grieve over a white thread that the dye would alter for ever, and at the crossroads Yang Zhu lamented the path's parting ways.

In Retired Emperor Horikawa's collection of one hundred poems, we read:

Where once I called on her	*mukashi mishi*
the garden fence is now in ruins –	*imo ga kakine wa*
flowering there I find	*arenikeri*
only wild violets, woven through	*tsubana majiri no*
with rank spring grasses.	*sumire nomi shite*

Such is the desolate scene that once must have met the poet's eye.

*

Nothing is sadder than the aftermath of a death.

How trying it is to be jammed in together in some cramped and inconvenient mountain establishment for the forty-nine-day mourning period, performing the services for the dead. Never have the days passed faster. On the final day everyone is gruff and uncommunicative; each becomes engrossed in the importance of his own tidying and packing, then all go their separate ways. Once home again, the family will face all manner of fresh sorrows.

People go about warning each other of the various things that should be ritually avoided for the sake of the family. What a way to talk, at such a time! Really, what a wretched thing the human heart is!

Even with the passage of time the deceased is in no way forgotten, of course, but 'the dead grow more distant with each day', as the saying goes. And so, for all the memories, it seems our sorrow is no longer as acute as at death, for we begin to chatter idly and laugh again.

The corpse is buried on some deserted mountainside, we visit it only at the prescribed times, and soon moss has covered the grave marker, the grave is buried under fallen leaves, and only the howling evening winds and the moon at night come calling there.

It is all very well while there are those who remember and mourn the dead, but soon they too pass away; the descendants only know of him by hearsay, so they

are hardly likely to grieve over his death. Finally, all ceremonies for him cease, no one any longer knows who he
was or even his name, and only the grasses of each passing
spring grow there to move the sensitive to pity; at length
even the graveyard pine that sobbed in stormy winds is
cut for firewood before its thousand years are up, the
ancient mound is levelled by the plough, and the place
becomes a field. The last trace of the grave itself has finally
disappeared. It is sad to think of.

*

One morning after a beautiful fall of snow, I had reason
to write a letter to an acquaintance, but I omitted to make
any mention of the snow. I was delighted when she
responded, 'Do you expect me to pay any attention to
the words of someone so perverse that he fails to enquire
how I find this snowy landscape? What deplorable
insensitivity!'

The lady is no longer alive, so I treasure even this trif-
ling memory.

*

Around the twentieth day of the ninth month, someone
invited me along to view the moon with him. We wan-
dered and gazed until first light. Along the way, my
companion came upon a house he remembered. He had

his name announced, and in he went. In the unkempt and dew-drenched garden, a hint of casual incense lingered in the air. It was all movingly redolent of a secluded life.

In due course my companion emerged, but the elegance of the scene led me to stay a little longer and watch from the shadows. Soon the double doors opened a fraction wider; it seemed the lady was gazing at the moon. It would have been very disappointing had she immediately bolted the doors as soon as the visit was over. She could not know that someone would still be watching. Such sensibility could only be the fruit of a habitual attitude of mind.

I heard that this lady died not long after.

*

It is foolish to be in thrall to fame and fortune, engaged in painful striving all your life with never a moment of peace and tranquillity.

Great wealth will drive you to neglect your own well-being in pursuit of it. It is asking for harm and tempting trouble. Though you leave behind at your death a mountain of gold high enough to prop up the North Star itself, it will only cause problems for those who come after you. Nor is there any point in all those pleasures that delight the eyes of fools. Big carriages, fat horses, glittering gold and jewels – any man of sensibility would view such things as gross stupidity. Toss your gold away in the mountains; hurl your jewels into the deep. Only a complete fool is led astray by avarice.

Everyone would like to leave their name unburied for posterity – but the high-born and exalted are not necessarily fine people, surely. A dull, stupid person can be born into a good house, attain high status thanks to opportunity and live in the height of luxury, while many wonderfully wise and saintly men choose to remain in lowly positions, and end their days without ever having met with good fortune. A fierce craving for high status and position is next in folly to the lust for fortune.

We long to leave a name for our exceptional wisdom and sensibility – but when you really think about it, desire for a good reputation is merely revelling in the praise of others. Neither those who praise us nor those who denigrate will remain in the world for long, and others who hear their opinions will be gone in short order as well. Just who should we feel ashamed before, then? Whose is the recognition we should crave? Fame in fact attracts abuse and slander. No, there is nothing to be gained from leaving a lasting name. The lust for fame is the third folly.

Let me now say a few words, however, to those who dedicate themselves to the search for knowledge and the desire for understanding. Knowledge leads to deception; talent and ability only serve to increase earthly desires. Knowledge acquired by listening to others or through study is not true knowledge. So what then should we call knowledge? Right and wrong are simply part of a single continuum. What should we call good? One who is truly wise has no knowledge or virtue, nor honour nor fame. Who then will know of him, and speak of him to others? This is not because he hides his virtue and pretends foolishness – he is beyond all distinctions such as wise and foolish, gain and loss.

I have been speaking of what it is to cling to one's delusions and seek after fame and fortune. All things of this phenomenal world are mere illusion. They are worth neither discussing nor desiring.

*

A certain novice monk in Inaba was rumoured to have a beautiful daughter, and many men came asking for her hand. But the girl ate nothing but chestnuts and never touched grains, so her father declared that she was too eccentric to be marriageable, and rejected them all.

*

When I went to see the horse racing at the Kamo Shrine on the fifth day of the fifth month, the view from our carriage was blocked by a throng of common folk. We all got down and moved towards the fence for a better view, but that area was particularly crowded and we couldn't make our way through.

We then noticed a priest who had climbed a chinaberry tree across the way to sit in its fork and watch from there. He was so sleepy as he clung there that he kept nodding off, and only just managed to start awake in time to save himself from falling each time. Those who saw him couldn't believe their eyes. 'What an extraordinary fool!' they all sneered. 'How can a man who's perched up there so precariously among the branches relax so much that he falls asleep?'

A thought suddenly occurred to me. 'Any of us may die from one instant to the next,' I said, 'and in fact we are far more foolish than this priest – here we are, contentedly watching the world go by, oblivious to death.'

'That's so true,' said those in front of me. 'It's really very stupid, isn't it,' and they turned around and invited me in and made room for me.

Anyone can have this sort of insight, but at that particular moment it came as a shock, which is no doubt why people were so struck by it. Humans are not mere insensate beings like trees or rocks, after all, and on occasion things can really strike home.

*

Those who feel the impulse to pursue the path of enlightenment should immediately take the step, and not defer it while they attend to all the other things on their mind.

If you say to yourself, 'Let's just wait until after this is over,' or 'While I'm at it I'll just see to that,' or 'People will criticize me about such-and-such so I should make sure it's all dealt with and causes no problem later,' or 'There's been time enough so far, after all, and it won't take long just to a wait a little longer while I do this. Let's not rush into things,' one imperative thing after another will occur to detain you. There will be no end to it all, and the day of decision will never come.

In general, I find that reasonably sensitive and intelligent people will pass their whole life without taking the step they know they should. Would anyone with a fire close behind him choose to pause before fleeing? In a matter of life and death, one casts aside shame, abandons riches and runs. Does mortality wait on our choosing? Death comes upon us more swiftly than fire or flood. There is no escaping it. Who at that moment can refuse to part with all they love – aged parents, beloved children, lord and master, or the love of others?

*

The holy man of Shosha had accumulated such merit through recitations of *The Lotus Sutra* that he had attained purity of the Six Senses.

Once, on a journey, he entered the lodging where he was to stay the night and heard the bubbling of a pot of beans being boiled over a fire made from their husks.

'We're so closely related and yet you boil us so brutally!' they were crying, and the bean husks crackling in the flames seemed to him to reply, 'Do you imagine we're boiling you on purpose? It's excruciating for us to be burning like this, heaven knows, but we're powerless to stop. Enough of these recriminations!'

*

As soon as I hear someone's name, I feel I can picture their face, but when I actually meet them no one ever looks as I had been imagining all that time.

Also, I wonder if everyone, on hearing some old tale, imagines it as taking place in a certain part of some house he knows, and identifies the characters with people he sees in life, as I do.

And is it just I who sometimes feels a conviction that what someone is saying, or what you're seeing or thinking just then, has already happened before, though you cannot remember when?

*

Unpleasant things – a great many things cluttering up the area where someone is sitting. A lot of brushes lying on an ink stone. A crowd of Buddhist images in a private worship hall. A large collection of stones and plants in a garden. Too many children and grandchildren in a house.

Too much talk when meeting others. A long list of one's virtuous acts in a supplicatory prayer.

Things that are not unpleasant in large amounts are books on a book cart, and rubbish on a rubbish heap.

*

What kind of man will feel depressed at being idle? There is nothing finer than to be alone with nothing to distract you.

If you follow the ways of the world, your heart will be drawn to its sensual defilements and easily led astray; if you go among people, your words will be guided by others' responses rather than come from the heart. There is nothing firm or stable in a life spent between larking about together and quarrelling, exuberant one moment, aggrieved and resentful the next. You are forever pondering pros and cons, endlessly absorbed in questions of gain and loss. And on top of delusion comes drunkenness, and in that drunkenness you dream.

Scurrying and bustling, heedless and forgetful – such are all men. Even if you do not yet understand the True Way, you can achieve what could be termed temporary happiness at least by removing yourself from outside influences, taking no part in the affairs of the world, calming yourself and stilling the mind. As *The Great Cessation and Insight* says, we must 'break all ties with everyday life, human affairs, the arts and scholarship'.

*

I cannot bear the way people will make it their business to know all the details of some current rumour, even though it has nothing to do with them, and then proceed to pass the story on and do their best to learn more. Wandering monks up from some provincial backwater seem particularly adept at prying into tales about others as if it was their own concern, and spreading the word in such detail that you wonder how on earth they came to know so much.

*

Nor can I bear the way people will spread excited rumours about the latest marvels. A refined person will not learn of things until the rumours are old and stale.

If someone new comes visiting, the boorish and insensitive will always manage to make the visitor feel ignorant by exchanging cryptic remarks about something they all know among themselves, some story or name, chuckling and exchanging knowing glances.

*

When someone complained that it was a great shame the way fine silk covers are so soon damaged, Ton'a replied,

'It is only after the top and bottom edges of the silk have frayed, or when the mother-of-pearl has peeled off the roller, that a scroll is truly impressive' – an astonishingly fine remark, I felt. Similarly, an unmatched set of bound books can be considered unattractive, but Bishop Kōyū impressed me deeply by saying that only a boring man will always want things to match; real quality lies in irregularity – another excellent remark.

In all things, perfect regularity is tasteless. Something left not quite finished is very appealing, a gesture towards the future. Someone told me that even in the construction of the imperial palace, some part is always left uncompleted.

In the Buddhist scriptures and other works written by the great men of old there are also a number of missing sections.

*

The Dainagon Abbot employed a young acolyte by the name of Otozuru-maru, who came to be on intimate terms with one Yasura-dono and was constantly coming and going to visit him.

One day, seeing the lad return, the abbot asked where he had been. 'I've been to see Yasura-dono,' he replied.

'Is this Yasura-dono a layman, or a monk?' enquired the abbot.

Bringing his sleeves together in a polite bow, the acolyte replied, 'I really don't know, sir. I've never seen his head.'

I wonder why not – after all, he would have seen the rest of him.

*

The Yin-Yang masters do not concern themselves with those days of the calendar marked 'Red Tongue Days'. Nor did people of old treat the day as unpropitious. It seems someone more recently has declared it unlucky, and now everyone has begun to avoid it, believing that things undertaken on this day will miscarry. This idea – that whatever is said or done on this day will fail, that objects gained on the day will be lost and plans made will go awry – is ridiculous. If you count the number of failures that happen on an auspicious day, you will find there are just as many.

This is because, in this transient phenomenal world with its constant change, what appears to exist in fact does not. What is begun has no end. Aims go unfulfilled, yet desire is endless. The human heart changes ceaselessly. All things are passing illusion. What is there that remains unchanging? The folly of such beliefs springs from people's inability to understand this.

It is said that evil performed on an auspicious day is always ill-fated, while good performed on an inauspicious one will be blessed by good fortune. It is people who create good fortune and misfortune, not the calendar.

*

A man who was studying archery took two arrows in his hand and stood before the target.

'A beginner should not hold two arrows,' his teacher told him. 'You will be careless with the first, knowing you have a second. You must always be determined to hit the target with the single arrow you shoot, and have no thought beyond this.' With only two arrows, and standing before his master, would he really be inclined to be slap-dash with one of them? Yet although he may not have been aware of his own carelessness, his teacher was. The same injunction surely applies in all matters.

A man engaged in Buddhist practice will tell himself at night that there is always the morning, or in the morning will anticipate the night, always intending to make more effort later. And if such are your days, how much less aware must you be of the passing moment's indolence. Why should it be so difficult to carry something out right now when you think of it, to seize the instant?

*

Someone told the following tale. A man sells an ox. The buyer says he will come in the morning to pay and take the beast. But during the night, the ox dies. 'The buyer thus gained, while the seller lost,' he concluded.

But a bystander remarked, 'The owner did indeed lose on the transaction, but he profited greatly in another way. Let me tell you why. Living creatures have no knowledge of the nearness of death. Such was the ox, and such too are we humans. As it happened, the ox died that night; as it happened, the owner lived on. One day's life is more precious than a fortune's worth of money, while an ox's worth weighs no more than a goose feather. One cannot say that a man who gains a fortune while losing a coin or two has made a loss.'

Everyone laughed at this. 'That reasoning doesn't only apply to the owner of the ox,' they scoffed.

The man went on. 'Well then, if people hate death they should love life. Should we not relish each day the joy of survival? Fools forget this – they go striving after other enjoyments, cease to appreciate the fortune they have and risk all to lay their hands on fresh wealth. Their desires are never sated. There is a deep contradiction in failing to enjoy life and yet fearing death when faced with it. It is because they have no fear of death that people fail to enjoy life – no, not that they don't fear it, but rather they forget its nearness. Of course, it must be said that the ultimate gain lies in transcending the relative world with its distinction between life and death.'

At this, everyone jeered more than ever.

*

A lady who had reason to withdraw from the world for a time had retired to a lonely tumbledown house, where she was idling away the long days of her seclusion, when one dimly moonlit evening a certain man decided to call; but as he was creeping stealthily to her door, a dog set up a fierce barking. This brought one of the maidservants. 'Where do you hail from?' she enquired. The man promptly announced himself, and was shown in.

His heart was heavy as he took in his forlorn surroundings. How must she spend her time here? He stood hesitating on the veranda's rough wooden boards. 'This way,' came a wonderfully serene and youthful voice, so he slid open the door with some difficulty and entered.

The place was not so shabby after all, but was modest and refined. At the far end a lamp shone softly, revealing the beauty of the furnishings, and the scent of incense lit some time earlier imbued the place with an evocative and beguiling air.

He heard orders being given among the servants – 'Take care to lock the gate. It may rain. Put the carriage under the shelter of the gate roof' – and talk of where his retainers should spend the night. Then one added, in a soft murmur that nevertheless reached his ears because he was quite close, 'Tonight at least we can sleep easy.'

The two spoke together of all that had happened since

they last met, until the first cock crowed while it was yet night. On they talked earnestly, of matters past and to come, and now the cock's crow was loud and persistent. The day must by now have dawned, he thought, but this was not a place he must hasten to leave before light, so he lingered on a little, until sunlight whitened the cracks in the door. At last, with promises not to forget her, he departed.

Recalling the enchanting scene, he remembers how beautifully green the trees and garden plants glowed in that early summer daybreak, and even now, whenever he passes the house, he turns to gaze until the great camphor tree in the garden is lost to sight.

*

A man famed for his tree-climbing skills once directed another to climb a tall tree and cut branches. While the fellow was precariously balanced aloft, the tree-climber watched without a word, but when he was descending and had reached the height of the eaves the expert called to him, 'Careful how you go! Take care coming down!'

'Why do you say that? He's so far down now that he could leap to the ground from there,' I said.

'Just so,' replied the tree-climber. 'While he's up there among the treacherous branches I need not say a word – his fear is enough to guide him. It's in the easy places that mistakes will always occur.'

Lowly commoner though he was, his words echoed the warnings of the sages.

Apparently one of the laws of kickball also states that if you relax after achieving a difficult kick, this is the moment when the ball will always fall to the ground.

*

There are seven types of people one should not have as a friend.

The first is an exalted and high-ranking person. The second, somebody young. The third, anyone strong and in perfect health. The fourth, a man who loves drink. The fifth, a brave and daring warrior. The sixth, a liar. The seventh, an avaricious man.

The three to choose as friends are – one who gives gifts, a doctor and a wise man.

*

The domestic animals are the horse and the ox. It is a shame to tether the poor things and make them suffer, but it can't be helped, since they are indispensable to us. One should most certainly have a dog, as they are better than men at guarding the house. However, since all the houses around you will have dogs, you probably don't need to go out of your way to get one yourself.

All other creatures, be it bird or beast, are useless.

When you lock an animal that runs free into a cage or chain it up, when you snip the wings of a flying bird and confine it, the beast will ceaselessly pine for the wild and the bird for the clouds. Surely no one with a heart to imagine how unbearable he himself would find it could take pleasure in these creatures' torment. It would take the stony heart of a Jie or a Zhou to enjoy witnessing the suffering of a living creature.

Wang Huizhi loved birds. He watched them frolicking happily in the forest, and made them his companions in his rambles. He did not catch them and make them suffer. We should follow the words of the classic: 'Do not cultivate rare birds or strange beasts in your own land.'

*

Grand Counsellor Masafusa was a fine, scholarly man, and the retired emperor was planning to promote him to Commander of the Guards, when someone in close service informed His Majesty that he had just witnessed something dreadful.

'What was it?' His Majesty enquired.

'I watched through a gap in the fence as Count Masafusa cut off the leg of a live dog to feed to his hawk,' the man replied.

His Majesty was appalled. The thought of Masafusa revolted him, and he was not promoted after all.

It is extraordinary that such a man would own a hawk,

and the story of the dog's leg is absolutely unfounded. The lie was most unfortunate, but how splendid of His Majesty to have reacted with such disgust when he heard the tale.

Overall, it must be said that those who kill or harm living creatures, or set them up to fight each other for their own pleasure, are no better than wild beasts themselves. If you pause and look carefully at the birds and animals, and even the little insects, you will see that they love their children, feel affection for their parents, live in couples, are jealous, angry, full of desire, self-protecting and fearful for their lives, and far more so than men, since they lack all intelligence. Surely one should pity them when they are killed or made to suffer? If you can look on any sentient being without compassion, you are less than human.

*

Yan Hui's firm belief was that he must avoid burdening others. One should not cause suffering and pain to others, nor undermine the will of the humble man.

Some will take pleasure in deceiving, frightening or mocking little children. Adults treat such tales lightly, knowing that they are quite unfounded, but those words will strike deep into the heart of a poor little child, and humiliate, terrify or appal it. It is heartless to enjoy tormenting children in this way.

The joys, angers, sorrows and pleasures of adults too are all based on illusion, but who among us is not attached to the seeming reality of this life?

It harms a man more to wound his heart than to hurt his body. Illness, too, often originates in the mind. Few illnesses come from without. There are times when medicine cannot produce the intended sweat, but shame or fear will always bring one on, which should prove to us that such things come from the mind. We find examples in the classics, after all – think of the man who was hoisted up the Ling Yun Tower to write its signboard, whose hair turned white from fear at the height.

*

Should we look at the spring blossoms only in full flower, or the moon only when cloudless and clear? To long for the moon with the rain before you, or to lie curtained in your room while the spring passes unseen, is yet more poignant and deeply moving. A branch of blossoms on the verge of opening, a garden strewn with fading petals, have more to please the eye. Could poems on the themes of 'Going to view the blossoms to find them already fallen' or 'Written when I was prevented from going to see the flowers' be deemed inferior to 'On seeing the blossoms'? It is natural human feeling to yearn over the falling blossoms and the setting moon – yet some, it seems, are so insensitive that they will declare that since this branch and that have already shed their flowers, there is nothing worth seeing any longer.

In all things, the beginning and end are the most engaging. Does the love of man and woman suggest only their embraces? No, the sorrow of lovers parted before they met, laments over promises betrayed, long lonely nights spent sleepless until dawn, pining thoughts for one in some far place, a woman left sighing over past love in her tumbledown abode – it is these, surely, that embody the romance of love.

Rather than gazing on a clear full moon that shines over a thousand leagues, it is infinitely more moving to see the moon near dawn and after long anticipation, tinged with most beautiful palest blue, a moon glimpsed among cedar branches deep in the mountains, its light now hidden again by the gathering clouds of an autumn shower. The moist glint of moonlight on the glossy leaves of the forest *shii* oak or the white oak pierces the heart, and makes you yearn for the distant capital and a friend of true sensibility to share the moment with you.

Are blossoms and the moon merely things to be gazed at with the eye? No, it brings more contentment and delight to stay inside the house in spring and, there in your bedroom, let your heart go out to the unseen moonlit night.

The man of quality never appears entranced by anything; he savours things with a casual air. Country bumpkins, however, take flamboyant pleasure in everything. They will wriggle their way in through the crowd and stand there endlessly gaping up at the blossoms, sit about under the trees drinking sake and indulging in linked verse-making together and, finally, oafishly break off great branches of blossom to carry away. They will dip their hands and feet into clear spring water, get down to stand in unsullied snow and leave their footprints everywhere, and in short throw themselves into everything with uninhibited glee.

I have observed such people behaving quite astonishingly when they came to see the Kamo festival. Declaring that the procession was horribly late so there was no point in hanging around on the viewing stand, a group retired to a house behind the stands and settled down to eat, drink and play *go* and *sugoroku*, leaving one of their number back on the stand to keep watch. 'It's coming by!' he shouted, whereupon they all leaped frantically to their feet and dashed back, elbowing each other out of the way as they scrambled up, nearly tumbling off in their eagerness to thrust aside the blinds for a better look, jostling for position and craning to miss nothing, and commenting volubly on everything they saw. Then, when that section of the procession had passed, off they went again, declaring they'd be back for the next one. They were clearly only there to see the spectacle.

The upper echelons from the capital, on the other hand, will sit there dozing without so much as a glance at the scene. Young gentlemen of lesser rank are constantly rising to wait on their superiors, while those seated in the back rows never rudely lean forward, and no one goes out of his way to watch as the procession passes.

On the day of the festival everything is elegantly strewn with the emblematic *aoi* leaves, and even before dawn the carriages quietly begin to arrive to secure a good viewing position, everyone intrigued about which carriage is whose, sometimes identifying them by an accompanying servant or ox-boy they recognize. It is endlessly fascinating to watch the carriages come and go, some charming, others more showy. By the time evening draws in, all those rows of carriages and the people who were crammed into the stands have disappeared, and hardly a soul is left. Once the chaos of departing carriages is over, the blinds and matting are taken down from the stands as you watch, and the place is left bare and forlorn, moving you to a poignant sense of the brevity of worldly things. It is this that is the real point of seeing the festival.

Among the people coming and going in front of the stands there are many you recognize, making you realize there are not really so many people in this world. Even if you were destined to die after all these others, clearly your own death cannot be far away. When a large vessel filled with water is pierced with a tiny hole, though each drop is small it will go on relentlessly leaking until soon the vessel is empty. The city is filled with people, but not a day would go by without someone dying. And is it only one or two a day? There are times when the corpses on the pyres of Toribe, Funaoka and elsewhere further afield are piled high, but no day passes without a funeral. And so the coffin sellers no sooner make one than it is sold. Be they young, be they strong, the time of death comes upon all unawares. It is an extraordinary miracle that we have escaped it until now. Can we ever, even briefly, have peace of mind in this world?

It is like the game of *mamakodate*, played with *sugoroku* pieces, in which no one knows which in the line of pieces will be removed next – when the count is made and a piece is taken, the rest seem to have escaped, but the count goes on and more are picked off in turn, so that no piece is finally spared. Soldiers going into battle, aware of the closeness of death, forget their home and their own safety. And it is sheer folly for a man who lives secluded from the world in his lowly hut, spending his days in idle delight in his garden, to pass off such matters as irrelevant to himself. Do you imagine that the enemy Impermanence will not come forcing its way into your peaceful mountain retreat? The recluse faces death as surely as the soldier setting forth to battle.

*

A sensible man will not die leaving valuables behind. A collection of vulgar objects looks bad, while good ones will suggest a futile attachment to worldly things. And it is even more unfortunate to leave behind a vast accumulation. There will be ugly fights over it after your death, with everyone determined to get things for himself. If you plan to leave something to a particular person, you should pass it on while you are still alive.

Some things are necessary for day-to-day living, but one should have nothing else.

*

Even people who seem to lack any finer feelings will sometimes say something impressive.

An alarming-looking ruffian from the eastern provinces once turned to the man beside him and asked if he had any children. 'Not one,' the man replied.

'Well then,' said the Easterner, 'you'll not know what true depth of feeling is. It frightens me to think of a man unacquainted with tenderness. It's having your own children that brings home to you the poignant beauty of life.'

This is indeed true. Without familial love, would such a man as this be able to feel compassion? Even a man who lacks all filial piety will discover how a parent feels when he himself has children.

It is wrong for a man who has taken the tonsure and cast all away to despise those he sees around him encumbered with worldly ties, who go crawling abjectly after this person and that and are full of craving. If you imagined yourself in his place, you would see how he might abase himself so far as to steal for the sake of his beloved parents or wife and children. Rather than seizing thieves and punishing their crimes, it would be better to make the world a place where people did not go hungry or cold. A man without stable means is a man whose heart is unstable. People steal from extremity. There will be no end to crime while the world is not governed well, and men suffer from cold and starvation. It is cruel to make people suffer and drive them to break the law, then treat the poor creatures as criminals.

As for how to improve people's lives, there can be no doubt that it would benefit those below if people in high positions were to cease their luxurious and wasteful ways and instead were kind and tender to the people, and encouraged agriculture. The true criminal must be defined as a man who commits a crime though he is as decently fed and clothed as others.

*

The imperial bodyguard Hada no Shigemi once said of one of the retired emperor's guard, the Shimotsuke Novice Shingan, 'He has the mark of one prone to falling from horses. He should take great care.' Shingan thought this very unlikely, but he did indeed fall from his horse and die. Everyone then decided that the words issuing from such an expert in his field were divinely prophetic.

So just what was this mark? people asked him. 'He

showed all the signs by having a very poor riding seat, and favouring horses that tend to buck,' replied the guard. 'Have I ever been wrong?'

*

It is not good to call on someone if you have no particular reason. Even if you go with some purpose, you should leave promptly once your business is accomplished. It is very annoying if a visit drags on.

There is so much talking when people get together. It is exhausting, disturbs the peace of mind and wastes time better spent on other things. There is nothing to be gained for either party. It is bad, too, to feel irritable as you talk. When you don't care for something, you should come right out and say so.

The exception to all this is when someone after your own heart, whom you feel inclined to talk with, is at a loose end and encourages you to stay a while longer for a peaceful chat. No doubt we all have Ruan Ji's 'welcoming green eyes' from time to time.

It is very nice when a friend simply drops in, has a quiet talk with you, and then leaves. It is also wonderfully pleasing to receive a letter that simply begins, 'I write because it's been some time since I sent news,' or some such.

*

A young man overflows with vigour, things stir his heart, and he is prone to passions. Like a flung ball, such a youth courts danger and physical harm. Riches are wasted in pursuit of magnificence, then all this is suddenly abandoned for the wretched robes of the monk; he is full of fervour and fight, suffers agonies of shame or bitterness, and his fancies are constantly shifting from day to day. He will devote himself to women and pursue infatuations, or take his example from those who have died with no thought to their own safety or longevity, behaving with such reckless daring that 'a long life lies ruined', or let himself be drawn wherever his heart urges, becoming the cause of talk for many years to come. It is indeed in youth that we make our mistakes.

In age, on the other hand, the spirit weakens, we become indifferent and apathetic, and nothing rouses us. The heart grows naturally calm, so that we no longer act in futile ways but instead tend to our bodies, live free of discontent and try to avoid troubling others. Age has more wisdom than youth, just as youth has more beauty than does age.

*

There are many incomprehensible things in this world.

I cannot understand why people will seize any occasion to immediately bring out the sake, delighting in forcing someone else to drink. The other will frown and grimace in painful protest, attempt to throw it away when no one's looking or do his best to escape, but this man will seize him, pin him down and make him swallow cup after cup. A genteel man will quickly be transformed into a madman and start acting the fool; a vigorous, healthy fellow will before your very eyes become shockingly afflicted and fall senseless to the floor. What a thing to do, on a day of celebration! Right into the next day his head hurts, he can't eat, and he lies there groaning with all memory of the previous day gone as if it were a former life. He neglects essential duties both public and private, with disastrous effects. It is both boorish and cruel to subject someone to this sort of misery. Surely a man who has had this bitter experience will be filled with regret and loathing. Anyone from a land that lacked this custom would be amazed and appalled to hear of its existence in another country.

It is depressing enough just to witness this happening to another. A man who had always seemed thoughtful and refined will burst into mindless laughter, prattle on and on, his lacquered court cap askew, the ties of his robes loosened and the skirts hauled up above his shins, and generally behave so obliviously that he seems a changed man. A woman will blatantly push her hair up away from her face, throw back her head and laugh quite shamelessly, and seize the hand of the person with the sake, while the more uncouth might grab one of the snacks and hold it to someone else's mouth or eat it herself – a quite disgraceful sight. People bellow at the top of their lungs, everyone sings and prances about, and an old monk is called in, who proceeds to bare his filthy black shoulder and writhe about so that you can hardly stand to watch, and you loathe just as much the others who sit there enjoying the spectacle.

Some will make you cringe by the way they sing their own praises, others will cry into their drink, while the lower orders abuse each other and get into quite shocking and appalling fights. Finally, after all manner of disgraceful and pitiful behaviour, the drunkard will seize things without permission, then end up hurting himself by rolling off the veranda or tumbling from his horse or carriage. If he's of a class that goes on foot he'll stagger away down the high road, doing unspeakable things against people's walls or gates as he goes. It is quite disgusting to see the old monk in his black robe stumbling off, steadying himself with his hand on the shoulder of the lad beside him and rambling on incomprehensibly.

If drinking like this profited us in this world or the next, what could one say? But in this world it leads to all manner of error, and causes both illness and loss of wealth. Wine has been called 'the greatest of medicines', but in fact all sickness springs from it. It is claimed that you forget your sorrows in drink, but from what I can see, men in their cups will in fact weep to recall their past unhappiness. As for the next world – having lost the wisdom you were born with, reduced all your good karma to ashes, built up a store of wickedness and broken all the Buddhist precepts, you are destined for hell. Remember, the Buddha teaches that those who lift the wine glass either to their own lips or to others' will spend five hundred lifetimes without hands.

Yet, loathsome though one finds it, there are situations when a cup of sake is hard to resist. On a moonlit night, a snowy morning, or beneath the flowering cherry trees, it increases all the pleasures of the moment to bring out the sake cups and settle down to talk serenely together over a drink. It is also a great comfort to have a drink together if an unexpected friend calls round when time is hanging heavy on your hands. And it is quite wonderful when sake and snacks are elegantly served from behind her curtains by some remote and exalted lady.

It is also quite delightful to sit across from a close friend in some cosy little nook in winter, roasting food over the coals and drinking lots of sake together. And delightful too on a journey to sit about on the grass together in some wayside hut or out in the wild, drinking and lamenting the lack of a suitable snack. And it's a fine thing when someone who really hates having sake pressed on them is forced to have just a little. You are thrilled when some grand person singles you out and offers to refill your cup, urging, 'Do have more. You've barely drunk.' And it is also very pleasing when someone you would like to get to know better is a drinker and becomes very pally with you in his cups.

All things considered, a drunkard is so entertaining he can be forgiven his sins. Think of the charming scene when a master throws open the door on his servant, who is sound asleep next morning after an exhausting night on the drink. The poor befuddled fellow rushes off, rubbing his bleary eyes, topknot exposed on his hatless head, only half dressed and clutching the rest of his trailing clothes, his hairy shins sticking out below his lifted skirts as he scampers into the distance – a typical drunk.

*

The one thing a man should not have is a wife.

One is impressed to hear that a certain man always lives alone, while someone who is reported to have married into this or that family, or to have taken a wife and be living together, will find himself quite looked down on. 'He must have married that nondescript girl because he thought she was something special,' people will say scornfully, or if she is a good woman they will think, 'He'll be so besotted that he treats her like his own personal buddha.' The impression is even more dreary when she runs the house well. It is depressing to watch her bear children and fuss over them, and things don't end with his death, for then you have the shameful sight of her growing old and decrepit as a nun.

No matter who the woman may be, you would grow to hate her if you lived with her and saw her day in day out, and the woman must become dissatisfied too. But if you lived separately and sometimes visited her, your feelings for each other would surely remain unchanged through the years. It keeps the relationship fresh to just drop in from time to time on impulse and spend the night.

*

What a shame it is to hear someone declare that things lose their beauty at night! All lustre, ornamentation and brilliance come into their own at night.

In daylight, one can keep things simple and dress sedately. But the best clothing for night is showy and dazzling formal wear. The same goes for people – a good-looking person will look still finer by lamplight, and it's charming to hear a careful voice speaking in darkness. Scents and music too are still lovelier at night.

It is a fine thing to see a man who calls on some great household looking his best late on an uneventful evening. Young people who pay attention to such things will always notice one's appearance no matter what the hour, so it is wise to dress well whatever the situation, whether formal or informal, and most especially at times when one is inclined to relax and unwind. Particularly delightful is when a fine gentleman has bothered to plaster down his hair though it is after dark, or when a lady slips from the room late at night to take up a mirror and see to her face before rejoining the company.

*

When the now-deceased Tokudaiji Minister of the Right was Superintendent of Police, he was one day holding court at his central gate when the ox of one of the officers, Akikane, broke loose, got into the court room, scrambled up on to the Superintendent's seating platform and there settled down to chew its cud. This was deemed a disturbingly untoward event, and everyone present declared that the beast should be taken off for Yin-Yang divination to determine the meaning.

However, when the Superintendent's father the Minister heard of this, he declared, 'An ox has no understanding. It has its four legs which can take it anywhere. There is no reason to impound a skinny beast that happens to have brought some lowly official here.' He had the ox returned to its master, and changed the matting where the ox had lain. There were no ill consequences from the event.

It is sometimes said that if you see something sinister and choose to treat it as normal, you will thereby avert whatever it portended.

*

Nothing in this world can be trusted. Fools put all their faith in things, and so become angry and bitter.

The powerful should place no faith in their powerful

position. The strong are the first to go. The rich should never depend on their wealth. A fortune can easily disappear from one moment to the next. A scholar should never be complacent about his skills. Even Confucius did not meet with the reception he deserved. The virtuous should not rely on their virtue. Even the exemplary Yan Hui met with misfortune. Nor should those favoured by the emperor be smug. You may at any time find yourself instead faced with execution for some crime. Never rely on your servants to be loyal. They can rebel and flee. Never put your faith in others' goodwill. They will inevitably change their minds. Never depend on a promise made. People seldom keep their word.

If you rely neither on yourself nor on others, you will rejoice when things go well, and not be aggrieved when they don't. Maintain a clear space on either side, and nothing will obstruct you; keep open before and behind you, and you will be unimpeded. If you let yourself be hemmed in, you can be squeezed to breaking point. Without care and flexibility in your dealings with the world, you will find yourself in conflict and be damaged, while if you live calmly and serenely, not a hair on your head will come to harm.

Humans are the most miraculous and exalted of all things in heaven and earth. And heaven and earth are boundless. How, then, could we differ in essence? If our spirit is open and boundless, neither fear nor joy will obstruct it, and we will remain untroubled by the world.

*

There is a place in Tamba called Izumo, where the deity of the great Izumo Shrine has been installed in a magnificent shrine building. The area is ruled by a certain Shida, who one autumn invited a great many people, including the holy man Shōkai. 'Come and pray to Izumo,' he said, 'and let us feast on rice cakes.' He led them to the shrine, and every one of them prayed and was filled with faith.

The holy man was immensely moved by the sight of the guardian Chinese lion and Korean dog, which were placed back to back and facing backwards. 'How marvellous!' he exclaimed, close to tears. 'Such an unusual position to stand them in! There must be some deep reason behind it.' Then he turned to the others. 'How can you not have noticed this wonder?' he cried. 'I'm amazed at you.'

They were very struck. 'Yes indeed,' they all declared, 'they *are* different from elsewhere. We'll tell this to everyone back in the capital.'

The holy man now wished to learn more, so he called over an elderly and wise-looking shrine priest. 'There must be some interesting tale explaining the placement of these images,' he said. 'Do be so kind as to tell us.'

'Indeed there is,' replied the priest. 'Some naughty children did it. A disgraceful business,' and so saying he went over to the statues, set them to rights and walked off.

The holy man's tears of delight had been for nothing.

*

He whose deep love spurs him to dare all and go to his beloved, though 'watchful eyes surround the stealthy lover' and 'guards are set to snare him in the dark', will leave them both replete with powerful memories of all the moments when they tasted life's poignancy to the full. It must feel very awkward and unromantic for the woman, however, if a man simply takes her as his wife with the full consent of the family and without further ado.

How dreary it is when a woman hard up in the world announces that she will 'answer the call of any current' so long as he is well-off, be it some unsuitable old priest or an uncouth Easterner, and a go-between sets about singing the praises of each to the other, with the result that she comes to someone's house as a bride without either knowing the other at all. What on earth would they say to each other when they first come face to face? On the other hand, a couple can find endless conversation in the memories of long hardships overcome, 'forging their way through the dense autumn woods' to be together at last.

It can generally be said that a great deal of dissatisfaction results from a marriage set up by a third party. If the wife is excellent and the man a lowly and ugly old fellow, he will despise her for allowing herself to be thrown away on the likes of himself, and feel ashamed in her presence – a deplorable situation.

If you can never linger beneath the clouded moon on

a plum-scented evening, nor find yourself recalling the dawns when you made your way home through the dew-soaked grasses by her gate after a night of love, you had best not aspire to be a lover at all.

*

The full moon's perfect roundness lasts barely a moment, and in no time is lost. Those with no eye for such things, it seems, fail to see how it changes in the course of a night.

An illness will grow graver as each moment passes, and death is already close at hand, yet while the sickness is still mild and you are not yet confronting death, you are lulled by your accustomed assumptions of a normal life in an unchanging world, and choose to wait until you have accomplished all you want in life before calmly turning your thoughts to salvation and a Buddhist practice, with the result that when you fall ill and confront death, none of your dreams has been fulfilled. Now, too late, you repent of your long years of negligence, and swear that if only you were to recover you would dedicate yourself unstintingly day and night to this thing and that – but for all your prayers your illness grows graver, until you lose your senses and die a raving death. It happens to so many of us. We must fully grasp this, here and now.

If you plan to turn your thoughts to the Buddhist Way after you have fulfilled all your desires, you will find that those desires are endless. What could be achieved, in this illusory life of ours? All desire is delusion. If desires arise within you, realize that they spring from your lost and deluded mind, and ignore them all. Relinquish all today and turn to the Buddhist path, and you will be freed of all obstruction, released from the need for action, and lasting peace will be yours body and soul.

*

The year I turned eight, I asked my father, 'What sort of thing is a buddha?'

'A buddha is what a human becomes,' he replied.

'How does a human become a buddha?' I asked.

'You become a buddha by following the Buddha's teaching,' he answered.

'So who taught the Buddha?' I asked.

'He became a buddha by following the teaching of previous buddhas,' he said.

'So what sort of buddha was the first one who began the teaching?' I asked.

My father laughed and replied, 'I suppose he just fell from the sky like rain or rose out of the earth like water.'

He used to enjoy recounting this story to others, adding, 'He had me cornered. I couldn't think what to reply.'